The 100th Day of School

By Amy Houts

CELEBRATION PRESS
Pearson Learning Group

toy animals

pretzels

rubber balls

Some schools celebrate the 100th day of school. Children bring 100 things to school.

Some children bring books to school and read 100 words from the books.

Some children count to 100 using counting blocks.

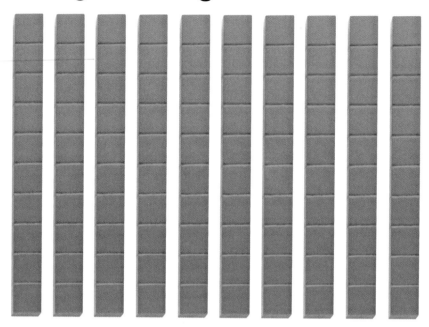

10 groups of 10 counting blocks = 100 counting blocks

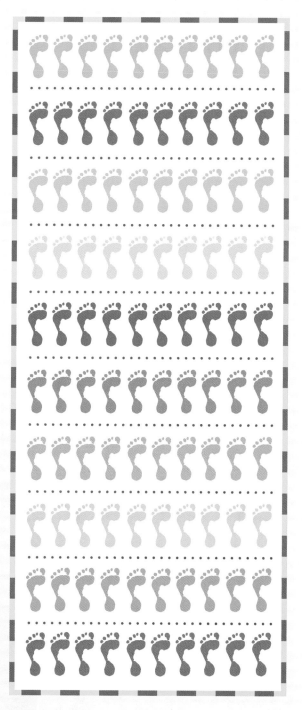

Some children count 100 steps while they walk.

10 sets of 10 steps = 100 steps

Some children jump and count
100 jumps.

10 groups of 10 children jumping = 100 jumps

Some children count 100 pennies on the 100th day of school.

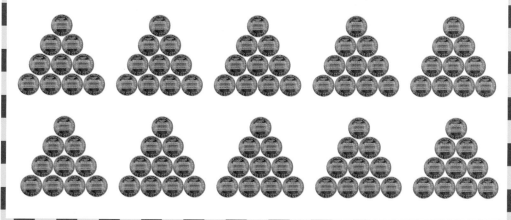

10 groups of 10 pennies = 100 pennies

There is so much to count on the 100th day of school.